OBJECT LESSONS FROM SPORTS AND GAMES

William C. Hendricks
and
Merle Den Bleyker

Baker Book House
Grand Rapids, Michigan

ISBN: 0-8010-4134-1

First printing, December 1975
Second printing, December 1976
Third printing, July 1979
Fourth printing, September 1981

Unless indicated otherwise, all Scripture references are from the Revised Standard Version, © 1952, 1946 by Division of Christian Education of the National Council of the Churches of Christ in the United States of America. Used with permission.

PHOTOLITHOPRINTED BY CUSHING - MALLOY, INC.
ANN ARBOR, MICHIGAN, UNITED STATES OF AMERICA

CONTENTS

1
ARCHERY

OBJECT: A target, an arrow or a bow

CONCEPT: Sin is missing the mark set by God.

TEXT: *Romans 7:7* "If it had not been for the law, I should not have known sin. . . ."

Most boys and girls know the story of Robin Hood. He lived in Sherwood Forest and went hunting with his bow and arrow. One day, he and Little John had an archery contest. They selected a target, and when Little John hit the very center, everyone thought he had surely won. But when it was Robin Hood's turn, he shot his arrow so straight that it split Little John's arrow exactly in half. The contest ended in a tie.

Archery is a sport that is growing in popularity. Some schools are including it in their physical education programs. Many people are setting up a few bales of straw with a target fastened to them for archery practice. What a thrill to put the arrow on the bowstring, pull it back, and make a bull's eye! Hitting the bull's eye takes skill and practice. You need to know about arrows: what kind of feathers are needed for the tail, what kind of tip to use, and how to balance the arrow. You need to know about fifty-pound bows and eighty-pound bows. That's how many pounds of pull it takes to pull the string back as far as it can go before you let the arrow fly *(demonstrate by pulling string back)*. The world's record for shooting an arrow with a hand bow is 856 yards. Do you know how far that would be? *(Select local building of approximate distance.)*

When you practice with a bow and arrow, you must have a target. In the target center is a black circle, the bull's eye, and that's what you try to hit. The colored circles around the bull's eye tell you how close you came.

God has given us a target too. It is His law. But each day as we try to keep it, we "miss the mark." That's what the word *sin* means—"missing the mark" that God has set for us. Each day God forgives our sins and shortcomings, but He does say, "If ye love me, keep my commandments" (KJV). These commandments tell us when we are pleasing God, or when we are missing the bull's eye. Let's try hard to do His will and to keep His commandments to love Him and to love others.

Can you make a bull's eye today?

2
MUSICAL CHAIRS

OBJECT: A few chairs

CONCEPT: Jesus has promised a place for us in heaven.

TEXT: *John 14:1* "In my father's house are many mansions . . ." (KJV).

Most boys and girls have played the game called musical chairs. For this game you need a piano, a record player, or a tape recorder to supply the music. And you need to set some chairs in a row back-to-back like this (set chairs with backs to one another). All of the players form a circle and march around the chairs while the music is playing. When the music stops everyone tries to get a chair to sit on. Everyone is in a hurry because there is one less chair than there are players. That means one player will be left without a chair. That player goes out of the game and another chair is taken away. The music starts again and the game goes on. Every time the music stops, somebody is left without a chair. Finally there are two players and only one chair. The one who gets the chair when the music stops is the winner.

But being left out in real life *isn't* much fun! If you've ever been left out of a group of friends you know how hard that is.

9

Do you remember the Christmas story? When Joseph and Mary came to Bethlehem the night that Jesus was born they had to go to a stable because there wasn't any room in the inn.

Jesus once told a story about five foolish and five wise girls. The wise girls took extra oil and kept their lamps burning so they could go into the wedding feast. The foolish girls didn't take extra oil and they missed the feast. They were left out.

When Jesus told us about heaven He said, "In my Father's house are many mansions, if it were not so I would have told you. I go to prepare a place for you . . . that where I am you may be also."

In the game of musical chairs you may find yourself left out and that is only fun. You may be left out of some things in real life and that is more serious. To be left out of heaven for all eternity is the most serious of all. That will never happen if you believe in Jesus. He has promised you a place in heaven and He won't take the place away like a chair in a game. Jesus keeps His promises!

3
GLIDING

OBJECT: Model airplane (glider)

CONCEPT: To believe everything you hear is very dangerous.

TEXT: *Ephesians 4:14* "... tossed to and fro and carried about with every wind of doctrine. ..."

This is a little glider *(hold up glider)*. What makes this glider different from all other types of airplanes? You can see that this glider has wings like an airplane, but something is missing. It doesn't have a jet engine to push it rapidly into the air nor does it have a propeller to help it fly. This glider can fly even without an engine *(show how it glides with a gentle toss)*.

A glider must be pulled high into the air by an airplane. When they both are very high, the rope between them is unfastened, and the glider begins to float back to earth. As it comes back to the ground, it must be helped by the wind.

A good glider pilot looks for strong winds to blow the glider higher, because then he can glide for a long time. The record glider flight was made in 1972 in West Germany when a pilot flew 907.7 miles. If there's no wind, a glider flight is very short. If the wind blows on the glider from the left, the glider is pushed to the right. The glider needs wind to fly at all and it does whatever the wind makes it do—even when the wind blows it into a tree or into a lake.

Lots of people are just like gliders. Somebody tells them that to have money is the very best thing in the world. They believe it and try to get rich. On the very next day someone else says that money is bad, and to have fun is the most important thing. So they change their minds completely and then they furiously try to have fun in everything they do. Then someone comes along and says that everyone ought to eat a lot of food. So they do that too. They believe in the good things and in the bad things. They believe everything people say is true and good for them. That is dangerous.

A Christian should not be like a glider that is pushed around by winds blowing from different directions. He must believe what is true and say *No* to the bad. When the Christian believes what God says and says *No* to someone who is disobeying God's commands, then he will be very happy.

When you play with a toy glider and see the wind slam it into a tree, remember that to believe everything you hear is very dangerous. God's way is the only right way. You will never crash when you believe in Him.

4
FOOTBALL

OBJECT: A football

CONCEPT: The Christian needs a period of quiet time to receive instructions from God and to rest.

TEXT: *Psalm 122:1* "I was glad when they said to me, 'Let us go to the house of the Lord.' "

In 1895 the very first football game was played. Today football is one of the most exciting of all games. Boys and sometimes girls play it in the streets or in the park. There's tag football, where the player with the ball must be touched to make the game stop. Or there's flag football, in which a player must pull a flag out of the ball carrier's pocket. The roughest kind of football is tackle where the players must make the person running with the ball fall to the ground.

Each team has eleven players. One is the quarterback who makes the plans to win the game. Members of the team protect him or other players who may catch the ball. The quarterback can run with the ball himself, or he can give the ball to his fullback to run it for him. Maybe he will even pass it to one of his men running down the field. *(Pass the ball carefully to one of the boys or girls.)* The ball must be carried over the goal line at the end of the field for a touchdown. The team with the most points wins the games.

The important part of football is the part that isn't very exciting. There aren't any long passes, fancy catches, or interceptions. This is the huddle. After every play all of the players get together in a huddle to talk and catch their breath. The quarterback tells the men what they will do in the next play. Maybe he even calls a time-out to give his teammates more time to rest and work out a good plan.

Sundays give us all a chance to get into a huddle to rest a little from all the things we do on Monday, Tuesday, Wednesday, Thursday, Friday, and Saturday. We don't have to go to school. We have time to hear what God says to us. He wants to help us like a quarterback wants to help his team.

Sunday is one time Christians huddle, but it shouldn't be the only time in the week. Football players don't huddle only at halftime, but many times during the whole game. Every day there should be some time to stop what we're doing and listen to God's Word.

The football players are very glad to have huddles in the game. Everyone who loves God should also be glad to come to God daily and on Sundays to rest a bit and hear His plan for their lives.

5
MONOPOLY

OBJECT: Monopoly board and chance card

CONCEPT: God has a plan for every life.

TEXT: *Matthew 6:10* "... Thy will be done, on earth as it is in heaven."

Sometimes on snowy winter days or rainy days, we cannot play outside. It's just too cold or wet. That's a good time to play a game like *Monopoly*. Lots of play money and houses and hotels are used in *Monopoly*. The players can become very rich in this game.

Some people love to play *Monopoly* so much that they play for hours and hours. One time four men put on their swimming suits and played *Monopoly* at the bottom of a swimming pool!

In *Monopoly* a player tries to buy as many pieces of property as he can. If you and I played *Monopoly* together, and I landed on your property, I would have to pay you rent. If you had a hotel on Park Place, I would have to pay you over one thousand dollars.

Besides, the squares with houses and hotels there are squares with railroads and some that have the word *chance*. If you land on a square that says "Chance," there isn't anything to do, but pick up a card. Chance cards give specific instructions like "Go directly to jail" or "The bank has made an error in your favor; you get $100." You can't choose what the card says to do. You can only hope that it's good and not bad! Maybe we could say that it's either good luck or bad luck.

Many people think that their lives are like a game of *Monopoly*. Those people try to get as much as they can and hope that they can stay lucky. They are always afraid that by some chance they'll get sick or lose their jobs. If their luck is good, they are happy; but they always are afraid of what may be coming. They don't know how to control their lives.

The Christian doesn't have that kind of problem. He keeps working and planning for the future. He knows that if he gets something wonderful, it is a gift from God. But suppose his little son gets very sick. The Christian says, "I know that God loves me and will do what He knows is best for me." A Christian doesn't worry about chance or luck.

Are you worried about something that is going to happen this week? Remember that God knows what will happen and will help you. With God there is no good luck or bad luck. The Christian doesn't have to take a chance, he just trusts in God. Do you?

CHESS

OBJECT: Board and chessmen

CONCEPT: All people are equal in God's sight.

TEXT: *Galatians 3:28* "There is neither Jew nor Greek, there is neither slave nor free, there is neither male nor female; for you are all one in Christ Jesus."

A chess game is a lot like war. The red kingdom is trying to win over the white kingdom, and the white army is trying to capture the red army. The game ends when the king of either kingdom is captured.

Each side has two castles or rooks, two knights, two bishops, and a king and a queen on the back line with eight little pawns in front.

Chess was first played in India about A.D. 560. The Persians learned it from the people of India. The Arabs learned it from the Persians, the Spaniards learned it from the Arabs, and by the year 1100, people in England and France had learned it too. Today there are world championship chess tournaments.

Some people spend hours deciding what their next move will be. But one expert chess player played forty other persons at once! All of the chess boards were in a circle, and the chess expert went from one player to the next as he played all forty games at the same time.

When you play a game of chess, you want to save the king. You may sacrifice a knight or a bishop to save the king. You may even plan to give up some of your pawns to capture a more important piece of the enemy. You don't consider the life of one little pawn very important if you can, by sacrificing him to the enemy, capture the king of the other side.

In real life, too, some people think they are more important or more valuable than others. Such people take advantage of others without stopping to think about what their actions will do to others. They use other people like pawns to get their own way.

God doesn't think of some people as more important or valuable than others. In God's sight there are no pawns and kings; instead, He knows that we are all sinners. He knows we all need a Savior. He commands us to love one another.

The next time you play chess and sacrifice a little pawn to save the king, the queen, or some other more important piece, remember that God treats us fairly and wants us to treat others the same way.

7
SKYDIVING

OBJECT: A small parachute made of a handkerchief

CONCEPT: Don't wait until it's too late.

TEXT: *II Corinthians 6:2* "... Behold, now is the acceptable time; behold now is the day of salvation."

When airplanes were first invented they weren't as safe as they are today. They had just one small motor with one small propeller. The pilot would sit in an open cockpit and from behind his little curved windshield he could easily look down to see the land below.

Wearing a parachute was important to him. If the motor failed, he could bail out and drift safely down to earth.

When airplanes were used in war, parachutes again became very important. If a plane got hit with an anti-aircraft gun, the crew members could bail out in time to save themselves. Some modern planes even have seat-ejector devices so that if something goes wrong with the plane, the pilot can push a button and be ejected out of the plane, seat, parachute, and all. The parachute will open automatically and he will float safely down to earth.

Today parachuting has become a popular sport. Some parachute experts even learn the free fall. They jump out of the plane and fall part of the way down before they pull the rip-cord that opens the parachute.

If you were going to jump out of an airplane at thirty thousand feet and had a parachute on your back, when would you pull the cord? Would you fall and fall and fall until you were just a few thousand feet above the ground? No, you'd probably open the chute as soon as you could.

Some people are like the parachuter who waits and waits to pull the cord. They go on through life without choosing to serve Christ. They are falling and falling—getting closer and closer to the time when it will be too late. What if they wait too long? The Bible says, "now is the day of salvation." Sometimes a parachute fails to open, but if you trust Jesus, He will never fail you. Only be sure to choose Him on time. If you haven't already chosen Him, do it today.

8
BULLFIGHTING

OBJECT: A red flag or piece of cloth

CONCEPT: Temptations are often attractive but dangerous.

TEXT: *Matthew 6:13* "And lead us not into temptation, but deliver us from evil. . . ."

A red flag means danger, doesn't it? If you are traveling along a highway and a road crew is fixing a bridge, a signalman may wave a red flag to stop the traffic. If there is a wreck on the road at night a patrolman may light a red flare to warn the oncoming cars. If a truck has an extra long load of timber or piece of steel on it, the driver will tie a red piece of cloth at the end so the drivers following him will be sure to notice it.

A cape made of bright red cloth is used by a bull fighter, but for a different reason. The matador doesn't want to warn the bull of danger. He wants to attract the bull's attention and get him to charge. He waves the red cape and quickly steps aside as the angry bull rushes past him. Soon the bull turns and charges again, missing by just a few inches the man who holds the red cape. The skillful matador knows how to wave the red cape to make the bull charge and he also knows how to stay out of the way of the bull's dangerous horns.

Finally after several passes, the bull fighter takes his sword and kills the bull as he rushes after the red flag.

You may say, "What a stupid bull!" Instead of rushing toward the red flag and ending up with a sword in his side, he should have stopped when he saw the red flag, or gone the other way.

Sometimes we are no wiser than the bull in the arena. We see something that we know would be dangerous to our Christian life or that would tempt us to sin. And what do we do? We go charging in, thinking we can easily win just as the angry bull seems to think he can easily gore the bullfighter. How much wiser it would be to stop when we sense spiritual danger, when we think something may lead us into sin, and turn and go the other way!

What do you do when you sense spiritual danger?

9
HOCKEY

OBJECT: A puck and hockey stick

CONCEPT: The Lord's work requires the participation of every believer.

TEXT: *I Corinthians 12:21* "The eye cannot say to the hand, I have no need of you: nor again the head to the feet, I have no need of you."

Do you know what this is? It's round, black, one-inch thick and three inches across, and made of six ounces of hard rubber. This is a hockey puck. When a good hockey player hits the puck with this hockey stick, it goes sailing across the ice. *(Demonstrate by hitting the puck a little way across the floor.)* One player passes the puck to another player until it is possible to shoot the puck into the goal net.

A goalie guards the net to keep the puck out so no score is made. If you have watched a hockey game on TV you know that the goalie wears a special face mask, arm covers, and leg guards. He has to be protected because when a player hits the puck toward the goal it may travel up to 100 miles per hour. In fact, Bobby Hull of the Chicago Blackhawks uses a left-handed slap shot that makes the puck travel about 118 miles an hour.

Hockey is a fast game. The players must be excellent skaters. They must be able to change directions swiftly and to stop suddenly.

Like all games, hockey has rules for the way it is to be played.

Because the game moves so fast, the players sometimes break these rules, and when they do, they are sent out of the game to the penalty box for a certain length of time. Normally a hockey team has six players, but if two of them are in the penalty box, that team has only four players left on the ice to play. A player who is in the penalty box can't do much to help his team win.

Some Christians are like those players in the penalty box. Such people dishonor their team by breaking the rules. They aren't doing anything to help their side win.

Hockey is a fast game. A player must be fast and skillful. Being a Christian isn't easy either, and the church needs every member. A church can't afford to have Christians harming the cause by sitting in a penalty box just watching.

10
BOBSLEDDING

OBJECT: A picture of a bobsled (a one-man sled)

CONCEPT: There are many times that we stumble and fall, but God our Father is always ready to help and save us.

TEXT: *Deuteronomy 33:27* "The eternal God is your dwelling place, and underneath are the everlasting arms. . . ."

Can you imagine going down a hill lying on your stomach on a bobsled going more than eighty miles per hour? That's fast, isn't it? I doubt that your Dad goes that fast with the car. In the winter of 1959, Colin Mitchell, using a little bobsled, flew down an icy trail on a hill. He went 83.5 miles per hour.

There are many kinds of bobsleds, but a one-man bobsled, like the one in this picture is the most exciting. (*Hold up picture for all to see.*) This sled isn't much longer than three feet (*indicate this length with your hands spread to approximately three feet*), and it doesn't have a steering wheel or brakes!

The bobsled must go on a very special trail with some straight parts, but also many curves. The workmen are careful to make the trail very smooth and icy. The bobsleds streak along these trails. The first one to get to the bottom wins.

How does a bobsled turn without a steering wheel? Well, the rider must lean to one side or the other to make it turn. He must drag his feet to stop the sled. When these sleds go too fast, they can't turn quickly enough. Then they go straight at a curve and crash. So at the most dangerous curves the workmen spread lots of nice, soft straw. Then if a sled misses the curve and crashes, the man won't be hurt.

The Bible tells us that God is our Father. That means that we are His children. Would your father want you to get hurt? *(Give time to answer.)* Of course not. When you were little and just learning to walk, your mommy and daddy held their arms around you. They didn't touch you, but if you started to fall, you always fell into their arms. That's just like the bobsled which lands in the soft straw.

God protects us like that. He doesn't want us to get hurt. Sometimes we like to do things by ourselves. We think we don't need God. When we don't ask God to help us be good, then we get into trouble. He wants us to follow His trail and to obey Him. If we should lie, cheat, or steal, then we fall into sin and we crash like a bobsled that missed a curve.

At times we all miss the trail that God has for us. But if we say that we are sorry, God forgives us. God sent us Jesus and He picks us up.

11

WEIGHTLIFTING

OBJECT: A weight or dumbbell

CONCEPT: God has given everyone certain talents and abilities which must be used.

TEXT: *Matthew 25:21* "... Well done, good and faithful servant; you have been faithful over a little, I will set you over much. ..."

Have you ever seen on TV a contest of strong men lifting heavy bars and weights? The men certainly have strong arm and leg muscles. Paul Anderson was the strongest man to live in the United States. One time he lifted 6,270 pounds. A very large car weighs only 5,600 pounds. He was a very, very strong man. I'm sure almost all of you wish you were that strong.

You can become very strong, but that does take a lot of practice. You can buy a regulation set of weights and exercise with them. If you can't get weights from a store, you can build some yourself with a piece of pipe, two tin cans and a little cement. Then with the weights you can exercise (*lift and lower the weights several times*).

If you want to become strong, you must begin with light weights or you may hurt yourself. Gradually, as your muscles become stronger, you can put more and more weight on the bar. After a time you will be able to lift very heavy things.

All of us have muscles in our arms and legs. All of us have exactly the same number of muscles as Paul Anderson has, but our muscles will not grow strong unless they are used and exercised. God has also given each of us talents and skills. If we do not use these abilities we will be very, very weak Christians. Finally we will not be able to do anything and we become sick Christians.

God wants us to use our talents. The more these talents are used, the better and more useful they will become. Probably none of us will ever be able to lift the weight Paul Anderson did, but we can exercise every talent received from God and use our talents to work for God.

12
SORRY

OBJECT: The game board of *Sorry* and a *Sorry* card

CONCEPT: It is very important to mean every word of an apology.

TEXT: *I Samuel 24:2* "Saul took 3000 chosen men . . . and went to seek David."

24:17 "Saul said to David, 'You are more righteous than I; for you have repaid me good, whereas I have repaid you evil.' "

26:2 "Saul arose . . . with 3000 chosen men of Israel to seek David. . . ."

26:21 "Then Saul said, 'I have done wrong, return, my son David. For I will no more do you harm. . . .' "

Many boys and girls like to play *Sorry* and, as a matter of fact, so do their moms and dads. It's an easy game to play. The idea is to move all four of your men from the starting point to the goal which is all the way around the board *(demonstrate this journey on the board)*. In order to get around the board, the players must pick cards and follow the instructions. Some

29

cards tell the player to go back four spaces, others say to go ahead two spaces and draw again.

An interesting card in this game is the *Sorry* card *(show it)*. With such a card you knock one of the other players' men off the board, send him back, and put your man in the spot he occupied. Maybe he was almost to the goal but that doesn't matter. You say, "I'm sorry" and send him back anyway. You don't really feel very sorry for him because now he can't beat you. Very likely you can beat him (if he doesn't draw a *Sorry* card).

"I'm sorry." How easy that is to say! If you really mean what you say, you add that you will never do it again. Then you would try hard never to do the same thing again. Let's say that you broke your sister's favorite toy. If you were really sorry about it, you would try to get another one to replace it and be careful not to break another one of her toys.

Lots of people say "I'm sorry" but don't mean it. They may say "I'm sorry," so that nobody will be angry with them, but then they don't try very hard to change. The next time they do the same thing again. King Saul in the Old Testament tried to kill David. Then Saul told David that he was sorry. But a short time later Saul went out to hunt David again in order to kill him. He didn't really mean his first "I'm sorry" nor his second.

When Christian boys and girls say "I'm sorry" to God because of something bad that they did, they really want to do better. They don't want to make God sad again. Nor do they want to make their mom and dad sad. When you say "I'm sorry," mean it.

13
MOUNTAIN CLIMBING

OBJECT: Rope

CONCEPT: Christians need each other.

TEXT: *Galatians 6:2* "Bear one another's burdens...."

Some people are afraid of high places. They don't like to climb up on a high ladder; they wouldn't like to wash the windows of a skyscraper or paint the ball on top of a water tower.

But other people enjoy high places. Some people especially enjoy mountain climbing. If you have ever climbed up a mountain trail to the top and overlooked the valley below, you know that standing on a mountain peak is a wonderful feeling.

Climbing up a cliff, where every foot and finger hold must be chiseled into a sheer rock wall hundreds of feet above the valley floor, takes special skill. Mount Everest is 29,028 feet high. A team of climbers first reached the top on May 29, 1953. It must have taken a great deal of effort and endurance to reach the summit.

Before a team of mountain climbers sets out on a climb, they gather special equipment, special shoes, special mountain stone axes, and some strong rope.

They use the rope to tie themselves together. Then if one

member of the climbing party loses his footing or falls into a crevasse, the other members of the party will be able to save him. It must mean a great deal to a mountain climber to know that he is not alone. The members of the team need one another to reach the top.

Christians don't have a rope to hold them together, but they do need one another in the same way that mountain climbers do. If some Christians are in need, others can help them by supplying food, clothing, or whatever else is needed.

If a Christian is tempted to do wrong and slips into sin, his fellow Christians can help to lift him up and set him on the trail to the mountain top.

Let's remember to act like a team of mountain climbers tied together with a rope. Let's help one another climb along the trail of the Christian life.

14
BASEBALL

OBJECT: A bat and a ball

CONCEPT: When a sinner is converted, his life changes. Instead of going directly away from God, he goes directly toward Him.

TEXT: *II Corinthians 5:17* "Therefore, if any one is in Christ, he is a new creation; the old has passed away, behold, the new has come."

The pitcher is a very important member of a baseball team. He has to be able to pitch the baseball accurately across the plate in the strike zone. If he pitches the ball below the batter's knees or above his shoulders or inside or outside of the edge of the plate, the umpire holds up his left hand and shouts "Ball!"

The best pitchers hold the ball in different ways *(illustrate)*. They make the ball spin and curve so that the batter will miss it. Another thing the pitcher uses is speed. A baseball pitcher can throw a ball at different speeds. When a really good pitcher tries to throw it as fast as he can, the ball travels over 100 miles an hour.

As the ball comes across the plate, the batter swings as hard as he can *(illustrate)*. If the batter hits the ball squarely, it will go sailing over the fence for a home run. Hank Aaron has hit more home runs than anyone else. Regardless of who hits the ball, something very surprising happens. A baseball that is going 100 miles an hour in one direction stops the very second that it meets the bat, and goes back in exactly the opposite direction.

Conversion can be something like that. Do you remember the apostle Paul? Before he was converted, he hated the Christians. He persecuted them and even had letters from the highpriest to go to Damascus to search for Christians there. But on the way, God not only stopped him but also turned him around and gave him a new direction. Instead of hating and persecuting the Christians, he became a Christian and the greatest missionary of all time.

This same thing happens to the heart of every Christian—by nature men want to go away from God, to disobey His laws, to follow the broad road to destruction. But God's Holy Spirit turns us around. His power changes us from going the wrong way to going the right way. The next time you see a baseball change directions, remember to thank God for changing your life so that you want to serve Him.

15
POLE VAULT

OBJECT: Piece of foam rubber

CONCEPT: In success and disappointment the Christian keeps on going.

TEXT: *Philippians 4:11, 12a, 13* "... For I have learned in whatever state I am, to be content. I know how to be abased, and I know how to abound ... I can do all things in him who strengthens me."

If you take a hard tumble, you can easily break your leg, your ankle, or your arm. Maybe this has happened to some of you, and you know it is very painful. With a cast on your leg you can't walk very well or do what you would like to do.

Athletes who pole vault, must fall a long way every time they go over the bar. After falling to the ground, they must get up and try to go even higher. In 1972 Bob Seagram used his pole to vault 18 feet, 5 and ¾ inches. After crossing the bar all these pole-vaulters fall on to a soft bag filled with air or foam rubber. This breaks their fall, and they don't get hurt. If Bob Seagram fell over eighteen feet to the hard ground, he probably wouldn't ever pole vault again. But he landed on the soft cushion and was able to try to go even higher. Look what a difference the foam rubber makes! *(Slap the table or pulpit with bare hand. Then put the foam rubber cushion between your hand and the table and repeat.)*

There are days when everything makes you happy and you want to laugh and sing. On those days you feel like you're on the top of a mountain with nothing to make you sad. Everything goes the way you want it to.

But some days are not fun. Everything seems to go wrong. Maybe you're sick on the day of your school picnic, and you can't go along. Other bad things can happen that make you unhappy. On those days you feel like you're in a very dark valley, and maybe you want to cry.

Everybody has ups and downs in life. Some people become so sad on the bad days that they give up completely. They don't want to keep on trying to do better. They are like the pole-vaulter who falls on the hard ground and gets badly hurt. He can no longer continue to jump and wants to quit.

The Christian ought to be like the athlete who falls to a soft pad, jumps up, and tries even harder. The Christian is going to have some sad and hard days. When these days come, he should believe that God will be near to help him. Then he can be happy even when the day isn't much fun and the landings seem hard.

Nothing happens to the pole-vaulter when he hits the pad. Immediately he's ready to get up for his next jump. If you're sad today for some reason, remember that God puts His cushion of love under you. He says, "I am concerned about you and will help you." He will help you to get back up.

16
GOLF

OBJECT: Putter or iron and golf ball

CONCEPT: The Christian's goal is heaven but his life along the way has many trials.

TEXT: *James 4:7, 8* "... Resist the devil and he will flee from you. Draw near to God and he will draw near to you."

"Fore!" That's the warning shout of every golfer who isn't very good at the game. He hits his ball, but instead of going nice and straight, it goes crooked and heads toward some people. The golfer shouts, "Fore!" so that these people will be warned to look out for a stray ball that's coming toward them.

Some people think that golf is a very silly game. The golfer hits his tiny little, white ball *(hold it up)* and then he has to go chase it. Finally the ball rolls into a tiny hole in the middle of a smooth, green patch of grass. But getting the ball into the hole isn't always easy to do, because the golfer must do it with only a few swings of his club *(demonstrate a swing—carefully!)*.

Every hole on a golf course is different. Some are short and easy, others are long and hard. Sometimes there may be a pond nearby with lots of water. If the ball lands in the water, it's gone, and the golfer gets a penalty. Another problem for the golfer is the sand trap. The sand is loose and if the ball rolls into the sand trap, it may be hard to get out.

Every good golfer tries to hit the ball from where he's standing to the hole without going into the water or the sand. If his shots are good, he can get to the hole easily without many swings. His score will be low and he will win the game. But if his shots are poor, he'll use a lot of swings to get to the hole and probably lose the game.

God gives to us the promise that we can live in heaven with Him forever if we believe in Jesus. He also promises to live close to us if we love Jesus. In fact, He'll live in our hearts. But Satan doesn't want us to love Jesus, to live for Him, and to be happy. He puts traps around us so that we can fall in and sin and make God unhappy.

Everyone who loves God tries to be good and is eager to get to heaven to be with God forever. But Christians must see the water traps and sand traps that Satan wants us to fall into. God wants Christians to follow His law. That's like swinging the golf club and hitting the ball right down the middle of the course toward the hole. That's also missing the traps the devil sets for us.

17
JUDO

OBJECT: A black cloth belt (2″ wide)

CONCEPT: We can't earn our way to heaven.

TEXT: *Matthew 18:4* "Whosoever therefore shall humble himself as this little child, the same is greatest in the kingdom of God" (KJV).

Would you believe that once upon a time, a long time ago in the country of Japan, nobody could own a knife or a sword? It's true. The rulers said that no one could carry any weapon whatsoever. This happened 230 years before Jesus was born. There were some bad people long ago too who tried to rob and hurt others. As a result the people of Japan began to use their hands, elbows, and feet to fight back and protect themselves.

That's how judo started. You may have seen on TV men and women dressed in funny, white clothes that look just like pajamas. They have no shoes on their feet. These are judo fighters who must practice a lot and be very smart. They must use their muscles and their minds *(flex your muscles and point to your head while stating this)* in order to trick the other person. This is why a little judo fighter who weighs only 90 pounds can easily throw down a big person weighing over 200 pounds!

When you start judo, you get a white belt to tie up those floppy pajamas. As you get better and better at judo, you get belts of different colors. After white comes yellow, orange, green, blue, and finally brown. The very best judo experts get black belts like this one. *(Hold it up, and then tie it around your waist.)* The experts wear their black belts proudly because they want others to know they are the best. The black belt is their reward.

The disciples of Jesus were almost like these judo fighters. One day while they were walking down the road, they argued about who would be the greatest in the Kingdom of God. If they had been judo fighters, they probably would have said, "I have a brown belt." And then another would have answered, "Yes, I know, but *I* have a black one!" They thought that they had earned important positions just like judo experts earn their belts.

Jesus called His disciples around Him just like you are around me this morning. *(This of course depends on the local situation. Perhaps it is impossible to have them around you. In this case say, ". . . like your mother calls you around her to read you a bedtime story.)* He said, "I don't give any of you brown belts or black belts. In fact, if you want to be the greatest in my kingdom, you'll never make it trying to beat others to the job."

You see, boys and girls, we can never earn big rewards in heaven. Jesus said that even we grownups must become like you children and love God like you love your parents and God. If Jesus is your Savior and mine, then we are going to live forever with Jesus. That'll be great, won't it. That is a free gift from God because He loves us. To get into heaven, we don't have to have a blue belt or a brown belt or any other sign of how great we are. Many people don't understand this. God told us all of this in the Bible. Now, do you think that we have to earn at least a black belt *(hold it up again)* to get to heaven? *(Let them answer.)* No, of course not! God has a better way.

18
MARBLES

OBJECT: A bag of marbles

CONCEPT: What we do is "for keeps." Time can't be turned backward.

TEXT: *Galatians 6:7* "Do not be deceived; God is not mocked, for whatever a man sows, that he will also reap."

In the spring, after the winter is past, yards and school playgrounds become dry again. The sun is nice and warm. Then lots of boys and girls like to play marbles.

First, you have to find a place that's quite smooth and then with a stick you draw the circle for the pot. All the players put an even number of marbles in the pot and then you toss your shooter to the lagging line to see who gets to shoot first. Your shooter is probably your favorite marble. Some boys call their shooters cat's eyes or aggies because they're yellow or blue. When you take a careful aim and shoot *(show how to hold the marble on your thumbnail and act like you're aiming)* you do your best to hit one of the marbles out of the pot. If you hit one out, that marble is yours. The idea of the game is to see how many marbles you can get.

When the game is over, if you were playing for points, the

one with the most marbles wins and everybody returns the marbles to the original owner. I guess that's the best way because then everybody has his own marbles back and nobody is angry because he lost his marbles or proud because he won them all. But not everybody plays like that. Some people play for "keeps." When you play marbles for "keeps" the player who shoots the marble out of the pot gets to keep it. If you put three of your favorite marbles in the pot and somebody else shoots them out they're gone. You may say, "I wish I hadn't put those in the pot because now they're gone." But you can't turn the clock backwards. No matter how hard you wish, you can't do over what you have done. Time moves on, and it's always for "keeps."

Do you remember the story of Jeptha? He was a leader and judge of Israel. Before he went out to battle, he vowed that he would sacrifice the first thing he met when he returned if God would give him a victory. Well, God blessed Jeptha with victory. When he came back, the people came out singing and dancing and the first person Jeptha met was his own daughter. How he wished he had not made such a rash vow before he left for battle! But he had made it, and couldn't change it.

Judas Iscariot who betrayed Jesus came back later to the temple. He threw down the thirty pieces of silver and said, "I have betrayed innocent blood!" But all of his guilty feelings didn't change what had happened—Jesus was crucified.

What we do is for "keeps." We may apologize for our mean or angry words. We may try to repay people for wrongs we do, but we can't take away the bad things we have said or done.

When you play marbles for "keeps," you think carefully about the marbles you toss into the circle. Remember to think even more carefully about the things you do and say.

19
ICE SKATING

OBJECT: A pair of ice skates

CONCEPT: The Christian life requires much work from the believer.

TEXT: *John 9:4* "I must work the works of him who sent me, while it is day: the night cometh, when no man can work" (KJV).

All of you know how easy it is to fall on smooth ice. Ice is very slippery, and the smoother it is, the more slippery it becomes. Smooth ice is dangerous to walk on, but that's the very best kind for ice skating.

Look at these ice skates *(hold them up)*. You can see each shoe has a sharp blade *(Point out the blade, showing how thin it is. Perhaps one or two of the children could carefully feel the edge.)* With these skates you can slide easily on the ice, go fast, and make some fancy turns.

The figure skater uses special skates with a thin blade to do his fancy tricks, jumps, and spins on the ice. The better he does in these things, the more points he wins. If he does very well and doesn't fall, he may win a trophy.

Every day Peggy Fleming spent many hours practicing to win

the world championship. In fact, she practiced four or five hours at a time on the ice with her skates just to become good enough at jumping, spinning, and turning with the music. She also had to spend many hours and days practicing to make a perfect figure "8" on the ice. The judges closely examined each figure "8" to make sure each circle part was perfectly round.

It takes a lot of hard work to become a good skater and many hours of practice are needed to develop strong legs and ankles. Even though sometimes we think being a Christian is easy, that too requires a lot of hard work and regular practice. It's easy to sit down and watch the ice skaters on TV, but we don't learn how to skate that way. Nor do we learn to be good Christians by just watching others do all of the work. Jesus wants you and me to be busy working for Him.

Jesus knew He had a lot of work to do for His Father in heaven, so He said that He had to be very busy while He had time. Jesus wants us also to do the work of telling others about Him. That means we must work and work hard, doesn't it?

Peggy Fleming spent at least five hours each day practicing to be a good skater. Are we hard workers if we only come to church on Sunday and do nothing else for God all week? What do you think? *(Let one or two respond.)* You know, you can work for Jesus by helping your mother or being kind to someone who maybe doesn't like you very much. You can even tell the Sunday school Bible story to your classmates in school. Ice skaters work hard to be good skaters. What do you do to be a good worker for Jesus? Begin this week to be kind to everyone, even to your brothers and sisters.

20
BOOMERANG

OBJECT: A boomerang

CONCEPT: The good deed will be rewarded.

TEXT: *Ecclesiastes 11:1* "Cast your bread upon the waters. . . ."

I bet you'd like to play with a toy that will come back to you everytime instead of going away from you. The boomerang is just that kind of thing. It's a thin piece of curved wood or plastic like this *(show the boomerang and its features).*

A long time ago in Australia these boomerangs were used for hunting. The hunter threw the boomerang, and it would sail out into the air toward some little animal or bird. If the hunter would happen to miss his target the boomerang would then spin around in a circle and return to him. The Australian hunters were very, very good with the boomerang.

Maybe you've seen these little, plastic boomerangs. Perhaps you've also tried to throw one, and soon found out that it really isn't easy to do. I can't throw it here to demonstrate because there isn't enough room. Anyway, today we don't use them to hunt birds or animals. We throw them just for fun and hope that they will come back to us. But we can't be quite sure because none of us is as skillful at throwing a boomerang as are Australian natives.

Did you know that the Bible says there is something which always will come back to you? This thing will never miss you. Actually, God is not giving to us some perfect boomerang to hunt with. He is telling us that if we do something kind to someone, we will receive a reward. Now this doesn't mean that we will be saved from sin and go to heaven if we do a good deed for somebody. Only Jesus can give us salvation. What the Bible does tell us is that if we are kind to others, most likely they will be kind to us.

I'm sure you remember the story of King David. He and Jonathan were very good friends. Jonathan helped David when he needed help, and David loved Jonathan for his kindness. If you say a kind word to someone who is angry with you, he won't be angry with you very long.

So, if someone does something to you that makes you sad maybe you should think about the boomerang. Be kind to him or say a kind and friendly word. It'll come back to you like the boomerang. You'll be able to be friends with him, or if that doesn't happen, remember that Jesus said in Matthew 5:12 that you'll have a great reward in heaven. Good words and deeds are like boomerangs that never fail. They always come back.

21
JACKS

OBJECT: A set of jacks and a small rubber ball

CONCEPT: The Christian life is exciting and we should want to tell others about it.

TEXT: *Matthew 28:19* "Go therefore and make disciples of all nations. . . ."

Do you know what these are called? *(Place the jacks on a table where everyone can see.)* They're called jacks. They're little objects with six points. You use them to play a game. It's played like this: bounce this little ball and while it's in the air you quickly grab one jack. Then with the same hand you catch the ball before it comes down. *(Demonstrate.)* Now, you lay that jack aside, and bounce the ball again. This time you have to pick up two jacks and catch the ball before it comes down. Then three jacks until all the jacks are gone. If you miss, it will be your partner's turn. The only way you can win, is to be *quick* enough to pick up the jacks before the little ball comes down again.

You know, sometimes when your father or your mother asks you to do something quickly, if it's something you don't like to do, you may obey so slowly it seems as though you are hardly obeying at all.

People do things quickly when they like to do them or are excited about what they are doing. Do you remember what happened on the first Christmas night? The angels appeared to the shepherds and told them that Jesus was born in Bethlehem. After the angels went back into heaven, the shepherds went quickly—with haste—to find the babe wrapped in swaddling clothes.

After Jesus had risen from the grave, when two of His disciples were on the way to Emmaus, Jesus walked with them. Later that evening Jesus made Himself known to them. Quickly they went all the way back to Jerusalem to tell the others they had seen Jesus risen from the dead.

Just before Jesus ascended to heaven He said, "Go therefore and make disciples of all nations." How are we going to do this? As slowly as we can, or as quickly as we can? If you are excited about the "Good News," you'll want to do it quickly—like picking up a jack before the ball comes down!

22
GYMNASTICS

OBJECT: A doll and a small box to be used as a gymnastics horse

CONCEPT: The Christian life must be built on a firm foundation.

TEXT: *Ephesians 2:19, 20* "... You are fellow citizens ... built upon the foundation of the apostles and prophets, Christ Jesus himself being the chief cornerstone."

How many of you boys and girls have hurt your head when you turned a somersault on the floor? How would you like to try jumping into the air, making the somersault, and landing on your feet again? *(Use a doll or other figurine to illustrate these movements.)* I wouldn't, because I might get hurt.

On television we can sometimes see a sport called gymnastics. The players turn somersaults and do other fancy tricks. They must be strong in order to do these tricks and not get hurt. Some of them are so strong that they can stand upside down on their hands. *(Illustrate with the doll.)* As these people do their tricks, the judges give them points. If they get lots of points, they have done very well, and if they get the most, they win.

Everyone who practices gymnastics uses a big heavy box with

four legs that is called a horse. That's a funny name, but the box helps them to do the somersaults and other tricks. They jump over the horse and use it to turn their somersaults in mid-air. Without it many tricks could never be done. The gymnastics horse is a very heavy box so that it cannot move when the gymnast uses it for his tricks. If it moved, he would fall and could get very badly hurt. *(Illustrate by pushing the box over and causing the doll to fall.)*

Have you ever trusted someone to do something and then discovered that the person changed his mind and didn't do it? Or, have you ever believed someone and later found out that he lied to you? We need to know what is true and then we can do things accordingly. If we believe what Satan says to us then we are like the gymnast who uses a weak horse that breaks. We are like the foolish man who built his house on the sand. When the rain and the floods came, his house caved in and was destroyed.

The Christian must be like the wise man who built his house on the rock. The wind and rain couldn't ruin that house. It had a good foundation. God gave us words to believe through the prophets in the Old Testament and the apostles in the New Testament. These words of God we can believe and trust. Jesus is the Word of God and we certainly can believe in Him. If we accept Jesus as Savior and believe God's Word we will be like a gymnast who has a strong horse that he can rely on. He will not fall because the horse moved or broke.

23
CONCENTRATION

OBJECT: A concentration game

CONCEPT: The prophecies of the Old Testament are fulfilled in the New.

TEXT: *Luke 4:21* "Today this scripture has been fulfilled in your hearing."

How good are you at concentrating? If you can remember well, and are good at matching things together you would probably win this game. *(Hold up game of concentration.)* First, you turn over one square *(demonstrate)* and then you have to find another one to match it. Let me try this one. No, it doesn't match but I must remember where this one is so I can find it back. I'll try another square? OK. How about this one? Does it match either of the first two? (If so) Do you remember which square it was? (If not) Which other one do you think it matches? *(Continue the game until you find the first two cards that match.)* To play the game of concentration you have to put two together that match.

The Bible is put together something like that. It has two parts, the Old Testament and the New Testament. And they match together perfectly.

Let me show you how this is true. Turn to these verses in your Bibles:

Malachi 4:5, 6 Luke 1:17   Elijah and John the Baptist.

Isaiah 7:14   Matthew 1:23 A virgin shall conceive and bear a son and his name shall be called Emmanuel.

Joel 2:28   Acts 2:17   And in the last days it shall be, God declares, that I will pour out my Spirit upon all flesh.

In the game of concentration every card has another one to match it. Did you see how each of the Old Testament prophecies we looked up has a New Testament fulfillment?

In Acts 1:11 when the disciples were watching Jesus go up into heaven, the angels said to the disciples, "This Jesus, who was taken up from you into heaven, will come in the same way as you saw him go into heaven." This prophecy isn't fulfilled yet, but it will be. We have to be alert, and we have to concentrate. We have to remember the promise, and we have to look for its fulfillment.

24
CANOEING

OBJECT: Paddle

CONCEPT: The Christian life is a life of work.

TEXT: *Philippians 2:12, 13* "... Work out your own salvation ... for God is at work in you both to will and to work for his good pleasure."

The longest canoe trip in history was one of 6,000 miles from New York City to Nome, Alaska. In the years 1936 and 1937 two young men paddled their canoe up and down the rivers of North America. Sometimes they even had to carry their canoe from one stream to the next in order to reach their destination.

The paddle is used to push the canoe through the water. It is quiet and does not pollute the air. Canoeing is a very popular sport because the paddle makes it possible to travel in very shallow water where other boats cannot go.

Once there was a young man who wanted to cross a river. It was a beautiful, sunny day. He got in his canoe, and using his paddle, he started out for the other side. In the middle of the stream his canoe began to feel the current. Soon he noticed that others in their canoes had thrown aside their paddles and were floating along in the current. So he threw away his paddle and settled back to enjoy the ride.

After some time, however, there was a distinct roaring in the distance. Neither he nor the others in the river knew what it was. Soon they discovered that they were approaching a deadly waterfall. The young man managed to catch a loose paddle on the river and, through a great deal of effort, paddled safely to the other side.

Sometimes for us life becomes so interesting and filled with things that look so good that we just drift along. We throw away our paddle, settle back to enjoy the ride, and do nothing. It is always easier to let others do the work.

But Christians have not been called to an easy, floating life. Drifting along leads to dangerous laziness. The life in Jesus must be a life of effort. It may mean paddling against the current. If everyone around you is doing something that is wrong, you shouldn't just float along and do it too. You must paddle upstream and do God's will even if you have to do it all by yourself.

25
FOX AND GEESE

OBJECT: Drawing of a large wheel with spokes

CONCEPT: Our sins make stains that only the blood of Jesus can wash out.

TEXT: *Isaiah 1:18* "Come now, and let us reason together, says the Lord: though your sins are like scarlet, they shall be as white as snow...."

(This object lesson is best suited for use in the early winter in areas where there is snow.)

One of the nicest surprises you can have on a winter morning is a fresh layer of snow. This beautiful white blanket covers all of the dirt and old leaves, and makes the whole world look fresh and pure.

But playing in the snow is even more fun than looking at it. You can make a snowman or have a snowball fight. One game that lots of boys and girls like to play in the snow is called *Fox and Geese.* You have to begin by having a nice big space of snow that doesn't have any tracks in it. First you start at one place and trample down a big circle like the rim of a wagon wheel. Next, you trample in some paths across the center from one side to the other like spokes in the wheel just like this picture. *(Hold up the picture.)*

After you have made your design in the snow, you're all ready to play fox and geese. As the geese try to get away from the fox who is chasing them, they must stay in the paths that are trampled in the snow. If they step out of the path, they are out of the game.

When the snow first falls there are no tracks, it's all smooth and white. If the boys and girls who play fox and geese stay in the path, all the rest of the snow will stay smooth and white too. But it doesn't take long and the path gets all messed up. Soon there are tracks everywhere.

Our lives are something like that. Each new day is fresh and clean. We have a track to follow—the way that God wants us to go. We are to love Him and keep His commandments. But it isn't long before we step out of the track. We fail to honor our parents; we say unkind words or do mean things. And once we have done wrong things, we can not undo them.

The Bible says, "... though your sins are like scarlet, they shall be as white as snow...." Jesus can forgive everyone of our sins. He can make our hearts as white and clean as the snow before it has a single mark in it.

26
BASKETBALL

OBJECT: A referee's whistle and a basketball

CONCEPT: A Christian can help to solve problems that others have.

TEXT: *Matthew 5:9* "Blessed are the peacemakers, for they shall be called sons of God."

I'm sure that most of you boys and girls know how to dribble a basketball. You bounce it on the floor like this, and then when it comes up, you push it back down. Up it comes again. *(Demonstrate.)* Just about everybody has either seen a basketball game or played basketball. You know that when you play basketball, you have to obey some rules.

If you are playing with your friends in the alley where you have a hoop nailed to a tree, or in your driveway, or at school, and somebody dribbles the ball with both hands like this, *(demonstrate)* or if he walks over to where the basket is and throws the ball through the basket like this *(act as if you are doing so)* everyone will protest. They will say "Double dribble" or "Walking with the ball." Sometimes boys even have bad arguments about whether or not a player broke one of the rules.

The game goes well if everyone knows and obeys the rules.

But even then a player can foul somebody or step out of bounds without meaning to do so.

The game goes best of all when there is a referee. In a real game he wears a black and white striped shirt so he won't be mistaken for one of the players. He has a whistle that he blows when somebody breaks a rule. The referee must know the rules. He must run along with the players so he is close enough to watch every play, and he must be neutral. If he favors one team over the other, the players get upset and argue, the coaches get upset and they argue, and sometimes even the crowd watching the game gets upset.

There have been lots of angry arguments in the history of the world. Cain was angry with Abel. Miriam and Aaron were angry with Moses. Joseph's brothers were angry with him. Saul was angry with David.

In the days of King Solomon two women were arguing about one live baby. Solomon asked for a sword to divide the living baby in half. Soon he knew who the real mother was because she didn't want the baby to be killed. He had settled the argument wisely and quickly.

In the Bible Jesus says, "Blessed are the peacemakers, for they shall be called sons of God" (Matt. 5:9). Christians should be busy stopping arguments. What do you do, boys and girls, if you see two persons arguing? Do you jump in and join the fight? What could you do to stop the people who are arguing or fighting? That's not always easy, you know! But Jesus says people who are peacemakers are blessed. You can't blow a whistle like a referee at a basketball game. You can't get a sword like Solomon. You can use kind words. You can try to keep out of arguments yourself, and you can help other people settle their arguments and live peacefully. Won't you try?

27
BATTLESHIP

OBJECT: A gameboard for *Battleship*

CONCEPT: The Lord searches our hearts and knows every·· thing that we do, say, and think.

TEXT: *Psalm 139:1, 2* "O Lord, thou hast searched me and known me! Thou knowest when I sit down and when I rise up; thou discernest my thoughts from afar."

Pretend that there are two little boys playing a game here in front of us. Listen to what they are saying and see if you can guess what it is. (Pretend to be two different boys in this conversation.)

"I bet you're in I-4, K-5, and in B-8."

"Nope, you missed me on every shot, but I know you're in J-9 and J-8. Maybe A-6 too."

(With disappointment) "Yeah, you got one hit! But you didn't sink me yet."

Can you guess what game these two are playing? *(Use your judgment on how commonly known Battleship is to them. If it isn't, give them time to guess but begin again very quickly.)* Yes, that is called *Battleship*. It's a game about a make-believe navy battle where one player tries to sink all of the other player's ships.

Each player puts his aircraft carrier, battleship, destroyer, submarine, and PT-boat on a board full of squares with numbers and letters. Here's the playing board. See the squares? Here are the different boats. Some are big; others very little. You are the only person who knows where your boats are placed. Then the shooting begins, and each player gets three shots at the other boats. To shoot you say "B-3" or "F-7". You have to have a good memory of where you shot so that you can sink the boats of the other players. In order to sink the aircraft carrier, you must hit it five times!

In *Battleship* it would surely help to know where your friend put his boats. Without wasting a single shot, you could easily win by sinking every boat. Of course, then the game wouldn't be very much fun, would it? It's more fun to search for the other player's ships.

God searches our hearts. He doesn't do it to sink our battleships, but rather to find out where we are and what we are thinking and doing. God can search like that because He is God. He knows everything. Think about it. He knows if you were good or bad this morning. Battleship players hide their boats. But even when we want to hide a lie we told, God knows all about it. The Bible says He knows when we sit down and get up.

If God knows everything we do, or say, or think, then what kind of boys and girls should we be? What do you think? *(Give them a chance to answer.)*

28
TREASURE HUNTING

OBJECT: A treasure chest

CONCEPT: To find the truth about God and His love for man is to find the greatest treasure.

TEXT: *Matthew 6:33* "But seek ye first the kingdom of God, and his righteousness, and all these things shall be added unto you" (KJV).

The saddest times you ever have are when you lose something. Maybe you lost your pet dog because he ran away. Or maybe you lost your best friend when he moved to another city far away. *(Pick a specific city quite some distance away yet known to the children.)*

But then some of your happiest times are when you find something that's worth a lot. How many of you have found some money on the street? *(Let them raise their hands.)*

Have you ever gone on a treasure hunt? A treasure hunt is a lot of fun because you can find surprises. Sometimes a map is used to point out the place where the treasure is hidden. Or, instead of a map, a list of clues is given to you. Let's have a little treasure hunt here in church. *(Before the church service plant two clues at different sites quite close together, with the* first clue telling where the second is located. Number 1 says, "Look behind the piano." Give this clue to a child volunteer. Clue 2 behind the piano reads, "The treasure is behind the pulpit." The treasure is the treasure chest to be used as the object) Let's see what this treasure is. (Put a piece of candy inside.) Look! Candy! It's yours because you found it.

I'm sure you've all heard interesting stories of pirate's treasures buried in some faraway island. The treasure chests are supposed to have lots of gold coins and much jewelry. Everyone wants to find out where the chests are hidden.

The Bible says that there's another kind of treasure we should all look for. The treasure isn't gold or silver buried by some pirates in a chest like this (hold up chest). No, the treasure is the Kingdom of Heaven. The Bible gives us clues about how to go to heaven. With God's help we can find the treasure. When we have Jesus as our Savior, we also get the treasure of living with Him forever.

Some of our treasure hunts may not give us a nice treasure, but God's treasure hunt will. I hope we all will find Jesus and eternal life.

29

DROP THE HANDKERCHIEF

OBJECT: Handkerchief
CONCEPT: We must always be ready for Jesus' return.
TEXT: *Matthew 24:44* "... Be ye also ready ..." (KJV).

(Hold up a handkerchief.) Do you know what this is? It's made of cloth and it's about one foot square. Well, it's a handkerchief. You know what a handkerchief is for, don't you? A handkerchief is especially important if you have a cold. A handkerchief is also used in one of the oldest games known. It's played by Japanese children, by Italian children, and by children in most other parts of the world. That game is called *Drop the Handkerchief.*

The players stand in a circle facing the center while the one who is *It* walks or runs around the outside. He drops the handkerchief behind one of the circle players *(demonstrate by dropping it behind yourself).* The players standing in the circle may not turn their heads to look until the runner passes them. He may go fast or slow to trick the players in the circle, or he may run at a steady pace. The idea is to catch the person by surprise when he drops the handkerchief behind him. Then the one who is *It* can get a good head start in running around the circle.

When the person in the circle does notice the handkerchief, he quickly picks it up *(quickly pick it up again)* and runs around the opposite way. If he gets back to his spot too late, he will be *It* next time.

To play the game well you must be alert. If the handkerchief is dropped behind you, you have to have sharp eyes. You have to be ready to act quickly; you have to be able to run fast. And you have to remember to run in the right direction.

As the runner goes around the circle everyone wonders, "When will he drop the handkerchief? Will he drop it behind me?"

Being ready in a game is important. It is even more important to be ready for the time when Jesus will come again. He said, "Watch therefore: for ye know not what hour your Lord doth come" (Matt. 24:42, KJV). Jesus told us He would come suddenly. "For as the lightning cometh out of the east, and shineth even unto the west, so shall also the coming of the Son of man be" (Matt. 24:27, KJV).

But you ask, "How can I be ready when Jesus comes?" Well, first you have to make sure your heart is right with Him. If you disobey your parents or teachers, or fight with your neighbors instead of loving and helping them, you aren't ready for Jesus to come again. You have to love Jesus. You have to ask Him to forgive your sins. You have to try to obey Him every day so that if He would surprise you by coming, you wouldn't be ashamed of what you were doing or saying or of where you were.

30
WRESTLING

OBJECT: A wrestler's head guard

CONCEPT: The Christian has enemies who are stronger than he is but God will give him all the help he needs.

TEXT: *Ephesians 6:12* "For we are not contending against flesh and blood, but against the principalities . . . against the spiritual hosts of wickedness. . . ."

To win a wrestling match you have to pin your opponent. That is, you must wrestle him down and hold both of his shoulders flat on the mat until the referee counts to three. One wrestler does all he can to get the other one down and at the same time he must keep from getting down himself. He uses all kinds of holds like toe holds and head locks *(illustrate)*. But to win, he has to overpower his opponent. In amateur wrestling there are careful rules about weight classes so that a contestant who weighs between 105 and 110 pounds wrestles with someone else in the same weight class and not against someone who weighs 200 pounds. Amateur wrestlers also need to wear a head guard like this *(hold up the head piece)* to keep them from injuries.

The rules for professional wrestlers are not as strict. It is possible to use more dangerous holds and cause serious injuries to win a wrestling match.

One type of wrestling in Japan is *sumo* where men who weigh up to 300 pounds wrestle for long periods of time. But whatever kind of wrestling it is, the wrestler who wins is the one who overpowers his opponent.

Long ago Jacob was coming back to the land of Canaan after he had worked for his Uncle Laban. He had worked seven years for each of his wives, Leah and Rachel, and six years for his cattle. On the night before he crossed the Jordan River, he wrestled with an angel. They wrestled all night. As it was getting light in the morning when the angel was going to go away, Jacob said he would not let go unless the angel blessed him. And the angel did bless Jacob just as Jacob asked him to do.

The Bible uses wrestling to show us how we are to fight against evil. We can never stop to relax, for then Satan will quickly pin us down. Just as a wrestler must continually exercise to keep his muscles strong, so the Christian must exercise his Christianity so he can resist evil with all his power.

Sometimes when the weak Christian wrestles with the strong and cunning forces of evil, we think he is pretty unevenly matched. We think that he doesn't have a chance. But listen to this little poem:

The devil trembles when he sees,
The weakest Christian on his knees

The Christian can't win with his own power but a Christian has God on his side and that gives him the promise of sure victory.

31
DODGE BALL

OBJECT: Ball (about volleyball size)

CONCEPT: Christians must work hard to get non-Christians to join their team.

TEXT: *Matthew 28:19, 20* "Go therefore and make disciples of all nations, baptizing them ... teaching them. ..."

If you can duck or jump aside quickly when somebody throws something at you, you would be good at playing dodge ball. To play dodge ball you need two teams. One team is inside a circle formed by the other team. A player on the outside circle throws the ball *(act as if you were going to throw the ball)* and attempts to hit a player inside the circle. As soon as someone inside the circle gets hit, he joins the other side, that is, he becomes part of the circle and helps the outside team instead. As the number inside the circle gets smaller, the number of players on the outside increases.

The persons inside the circle may dodge this way and that way *(demonstrate)*, but sooner or later, they get hit by the ball and must join the other side.

When the children of Israel were entering the land of Canaan, many cities were captured by Joshua and his army. When the people of Gibeon heard this, they quickly formed a plan so they could join the other side, the side of God's people.

When the twelve spies went to Jericho, they were hidden on the roof by Rahab. Later Rahab let them down over the city wall with a rope. Rahab had changed sides and was helping the enemy army. When the Israelites came to capture the city, they saved Rahab and her family. She later became one of the ancestors of David and of Jesus.

People who do not believe in Jesus are like the players on the inside of a dodge ball circle. They need to change sides. Christians can use God's Word, the Bible, to tag them. After a sinner comes to Jesus, he will join the church and then he will help his new team to win still more members. The person he is trying to win for Christ may dodge this way or that way. He may give all kinds of excuses, or go to all kinds of places to get away from God's Word, but a member of God's team must use all the strategy he can. Team members must work together until they win the person and get him to join their team.

Dodge ball is lots of fun. As you play it, remember that you need to work just as hard to bring someone to Jesus as you do to hit someone inside the circle.

32
TUG OF WAR

OBJECT: A piece of rope

CONCEPT: Ever since the beginning, Satan has been struggling to win control from God.

TEXT: *Romans 8:31* "... If God is for us, who is against us?"

Who has strong muscles? I need two volunteers who have strong muscles. *(Wait for two volunteers to come forward.)* Here's a piece of thick rope, and I would like to have you play a little game of *Tug-of-War* with it. When I say *Go* I would like you to try to pull each other over this line *(indicate a line on the floor).* The one who pulls the other over the line wins, OK? *(Give the two volunteers time to play the game. Hold up the hand of the winner. Thank both and ask them to return to their seats.)*

Tug of War is lots of fun, and it's good exercise. There must be an equal number of players on each side or otherwise it's not very fair. Once a year a college in Michigan plays *Tug of War* between two classes. Each class has a team. These two teams use a big, thick rope because the teams are very strong and have many members. In between the two teams is a river. A team must pull the other into the river to win the game. Of course, neither group wants to get wet, so they try very hard to win. Sometimes they pull against each other for over two hours!

Boys and girls can play *Tug of War* and so can teams of strong college men. These tugs can last for hours. But there's a very big *Tug of War* that has been going on for a long time. The devil wanted to be God. At the same time, he wanted the world for himself. That's why he wanted Adam and Eve to eat that fruit.

God wants us to believe in Him and to do everything that is good. Satan wants us to believe in him and to do everything that is bad. So Satan and God are in a *Tug of War*.

But God is stronger. He sent Jesus to save us from the devil, and God will win the battle. The Bible tells us that Satan will lose but right now he's trying to win. He tries hard to get us to join his team. If we do, we will surely lose. If we are on the Lord's side, we will win and will always be happy.

Be sure that you are on the right team.

33
HIDE AND SEEK

OBJECT: The pulpit or a corner of the platform behind which you can hide for a moment from the view of the audience.

CONCEPT: You cannot hide from God.

TEXT: *Jeremiah 23:24* "Can a man hide himself in secret places so I cannot see him? says the Lord. . . ."

If we would play a game of hide-and-seek right now, I wonder where a good place to hide would be? *(Look around a bit and suggest a few places.)* Now, if you were *It,* you would have to stand by the "base," close your eyes, and count to 100. Then you'd say: "Here I come, ready or not."

But I'd hide. Maybe I could hide here behind the pulpit *(move over for a moment so you are out of view)* or behind this corner of the platform.

Then if you went to look for me in the cloak room *(or some other place familiar to your audience)* I would run over to touch the base and call out "Free, free." But if you got there first and said, 1, 2, 3, for _____ *(use your name),* I would have to be *It* next time.

Playing hide and seek and finding a place where the person who is *It* can't find you is lots of fun.

Do you know who the first people were who tried to hide? They were Adam and Eve. But they weren't playing a game. They were trying to hide from God because they had disobeyed God, and they were ashamed and afraid. God didn't have to look here or there until He found Adam and Eve. Do you know why? Because God knows and sees everything.

Elisha the prophet had a servant named Gehazi. Once the rich general Naaman from Syria had leprosy. He came to Elisha to be healed. Afterward Naaman wanted to give Elisha many rich gifts. But Elisha refused. Then Gehazi followed Naaman when he was on his way home and asked for these gifts. Even though Gehazi hid them before he went back to Elisha, God told Elisha what Gehazi had done because God had seen it all.

Sometimes when we do wrong things we may try to hide them from our parents or from our teachers. We can never hide them from God who sees all things. But God has made a plan so that we can get in "free"—we can be free from our sins only if we believe in Jesus as our Savior.

The next time you play hide and seek, remember that you cannot hide from God.

34
BROADJUMPING

OBJECT: A make-believe flea cupped in your hands

CONCEPT: What little children do is also very important to God.

TEXT: *Matthew 21:16* "... Out of the mouth of babes and sucklings [infants] thou hast brought perfect praise."

You know what I have in my hands? It's my little pet flea. *(Look into your cupped hands and say, "That's all right, Oscar, I'll let you go free in just a minute.")*

Did you know that a tiny little flea is only about one-sixteenth of an inch long, but he can jump about twelve or thirteen feet? That's about two hundred times his length.

Now if a person who is about six feet high could jump two hundred times his length that would be over a quarter of a mile!

You know that's quite impossible! Why that would mean you could jump from _____ to _____ *(Use an example of two places in your community that are about ¼ of a mile apart.)*

Actually, the world's record is 29 feet 2½ inches for the longest broadjump. This record was set at the Olympic Games in 1968 when Bob Beamon from the United States beat the old record by two feet. This was a surprise to everyone and no one has come near that record since. That distance is four times his height. Remember how far my little pet flea can jump? About 200 times his length! That's fifty times better than a grown man's world record! *(Let imaginary Oscar out of your hands by opening them.)* "Oscar, just show everyone how you can jump." *(With your eyes follow an imaginary arc and go over to an appropriate place some ten feet away and pick him up again.)* "That was really great, Oscar!"

See, boys and girls, you don't have to be very big to do some great things.

Do you remember the poor widow who gave just two tiny mites to the temple treasury? Eight of these mites would make a penny today. Jesus noticed this poor woman's tiny little offering, and He said she had given the most of all.

And then there was a little maid who worked in the house of Naaman. You could ask, "What can such a little slave girl do for God?" Do you know that what she said about the God of Israel was so important that the rich and powerful Naaman went to his king when he heard it? The king sent Naaman to Israel where he met Elisha. God healed Naaman. See what happened when a little slave girl wasn't ashamed to talk about God?

No, you don't have to be big or powerful to do something important for Jesus. Just remember little Oscar here. *(Look in your hands and say,* "That's all right, Oscar, I'll let you out in a minute".) You can hardly see him, and yet he can beat man's world's record in broadjumping by fifty times. Remember, boys and girls, even though you are still small God can use you too to honor Him. Won't you try today?

Now, Oscar, I think I'll just set you free. *(Open your hands and watch him take an imaginary jump into the audience.)*

35
BOWLING

OBJECT: A bowling ball, two or more bowling pins

CONCEPT: Our lives affect the lives of others for good or evil.

TEXT: *Matthew 18:6* "But whoever causes one of these little ones who believe in me to sin, it would be better for him to have a great millstone fastened round his neck and to be drowned in the depth of the sea."

Lots of people in America enjoy bowling. Some people bowl for exercise and others bowl just for fun. A bowling lane is built with a little gutter on each side. The lane is only about forty-two inches wide and sixty feet long. So when you bowl, you have to roll the ball pretty straight. If you don't, it will go into the gutter and miss all the pins.

A perfect score in bowling is three hundred points for a game. To make this score, you must have twelve strikes in a row. A strike is when all ten pins are knocked down with one ball.

How can you knock down all ten pins with one ball when the ball is only about eight and a half inches wide? Well, when the ball hits one pin and makes that pin hit another pin, and that pin hits another pin, and so on until all the pins fall over, then you have a beautiful strike. *(Roll the ball against one pin in such a way that it in turn knocks down the second pin.)*

Many of the things we do are like those falling bowling pins. What we do affects the life of someone, and what he does touches the life of someone else and so on. For example, if you tell your friend about Jesus, and then he tells someone and then that person tells someone else, soon many people will know about Jesus. But if you tell a bad story to someone and he tells others, soon many people will know the bad story too.

Think about how one bowling pin knocks over another one near it and remember that what you do or say may spread out and help or hurt lots of other people.

36
RELAY RACE

OBJECT: One assistant and a baton or round piece of wood about one foot long

CONCEPT: Christians of all ages work together to carry God's kingdom forward.

TEXT: *Acts 1:8* ". . . and you shall be my witnesses in Jerusalem and in all Judea and Samaria and to the end of the earth."

A track relay team usually has four members. Before the relay race begins, the runners are spaced around the track so each has to run one-fourth of the distance.

Long ago, at the time of the first Olympic games in Greece, the Greeks had a custom that runners would carry a lighted torch from Mount Olympus to the place where the games would be held. The torch was carefully passed from one runner to the next until it reached its destination. This was a type of relay race.

In a relay race today, the stick or baton has to be passed from one runner to the next within a zone of twenty yards. Usually the incoming runner holds the baton in his left hand and passes it to the right hand of the relief runner. Every split second counts if the race is to be won. The runners are running side by side for just a moment and then one falls out and the other has a fresh start to carry on the race at top speed. This is the way it is usually done. I will need one helper today. *(Hold stick in your left hand as you jog up to your helper who jogs with you as you hand over the baton to his right hand as he runs off.)* Only if the baton is passed smoothly can the race be won.

Working in God's Kingdom is something like a relay race. There have been many, many workers since the time of the twelve apostles. One generation passes the torch to the next. We, like a relay runner, have to be careful how we pick up the message of God's Kingdom. We have to do this carefully. We can't drop part of it or leave part of it behind. Then we have to watch how we carry it. We have to be swift. We have to use our very best energy and effort because it won't be long and we will pass it on to someone else. We have to be careful how we do that too. The message of God's Kingdom has to be handed over to others so they can receive it and carry it on. It doesn't matter where we are in the relay race of life, we all have to do our best to keep the message of God's Kingdom in first place.

37
JACK STRAWS

OBJECT: A few dozen drinking straws or toothpicks

CONCEPT: In the church what affects one member for good or bad affects all of the members.

TEXT: *I Corinthians 12:26* "If one member suffers, all suffer together; if one member is honored, all rejoice together."

In gym classes boys and girls sometimes like to play pyramid. First, three pupils go on their hands and knees side by side. Then two others get on their backs for a second layer and finally one person climbs to the top layer and has one knee on the back of each person on the second layer. All goes well if every person holds up in his place. But if one person collapses—down comes the whole pile. *(Use your arms to demonstrate how such a pyramid would be built and collapse.)*

Well, the game of Jack Straws is something like pyramid, only it's played with straws instead of people. First you take a handful of straws and drop them in a stack like this *(drop the straws to form something of a pyramid)*. Then one player starts to take off the straws as carefully as he can. He has to do this one by one without causing any other straws to move. If he moves another straw even a tiny bit, he must stop trying and the other player gets to take a turn. The player who ends up with the most straws wins. Do you know what often happens? When you try to remove one straw, no matter how you try not to move other straws, they seem to roll anyway. Sometimes the whole pile comes down. If you touch just one straw, you really affect all the others in the pile.

The members of a family and the members of the church are a lot like that pile of straws. How? If one member of a family gets hurt, or gets sick, or gets into trouble, all the family members feel sorry for him. They do all they can to help. If a little baby is sick, his mother and daddy who love him very much may even wish they could be sick in his place. In church this is true too. If the members love one another and are concerned about each other, they will try to help each other because together they make up the church of God. They help to hold each other up just like a pile of jackstraws. What helps one helps them all. What hurts one hurts them all. I hope you care that much about the other members of our church!

38
JIGSAW PUZZLES

OBJECT: Two puzzles: one in a neat box with the picture clearly shown on the cover, and one with just some loose pieces in an old box without a cover

CONCEPT: God has given us some clues about how beautiful heaven will be, but we will not really see it in all its glory until we are there.

TEXT: *II Timothy 4:8* "Henceforth there is laid up for me the crown of righteousness, which the Lord, the righteous judge, will award to me on that Day...also to all who have loved his appearing."

Do you like to work jigsaw puzzles? I do. In fact, at our house if we set up the card table and dump a puzzle out on it everybody helps to make the puzzle. Everyone just adds a piece or two if they have time, and pretty soon it's all finished.

One little piece of a puzzle really doesn't give you much of an idea of what the whole picture is like. *(Hold up one small piece.)* You see this little piece, it's blue, isn't it? Now there are 300 *(or 500 or 1000)* pieces in this puzzle and from looking at this one little piece you can't tell if it's blue sky or part of a lake, can you? Here's another little piece that is brown *(perhaps you could pick up a piece that has lines on it or other clues which you could describe)*, now what do you suppose that could be a part of? *(You may wish to get various responses.)*

If you are working a jigsaw puzzle, it helps to have a picture from the box to see what it will be like when it is finished. *(Hold up the box with the picture on it.)* But here is another puzzle. It also has lots of pieces, but the cover of this box is gone. I don't know if all the pieces are here. I wonder what the picture will be like?

Sometimes, boys and girls, we wonder what heaven will be like. We don't really know exactly; it's something like a puzzle. The Bible has shown us many of the pieces of the puzzle:

We know that there will be no sickness in heaven.

We know there will be no more crying or sorrow.

We know that there will be no more death and that we will be with Jesus forever and ever.

We know it will be very beautiful because the Bible tells us that the new Jerusalem will have streets of gold.

All of these statements are like pieces of a puzzle. We can study the Bible to try to fit them together. We can get some idea of what the finished picture will be like. We can see some of its outlines and a little bit of how wonderful it will be. But we can't really see how beautiful it will be because we just can't fit all the pieces together yet.

We know, though, that if we believe in Jesus and love Him, some day we will see the finished picture. We will not only see heaven in all its glory, we will also be there to enjoy it and praise God there. Do you wonder what heaven will be like? Think about the parts of the puzzle that God has shown to us and look forward to the time when you will see it as it really is.

39
FENCING

OBJECT: A homemade sword about three feet long

CONCEPT: We can use the Bible as the sword of the Spirit to fight against Satan.

TEXT: *Ephesians 6:17* "And take the helmet of salvation, and the sword of the Spirit, which is the word of God."

This, you can easily see, is a sword *(hold it up, wave it around for all to see).* I made it of wood and it's about as nice a sword as I ever made.

Today some people use swords in a sport called fencing. Fencing started a long time ago when men used to fight duels. If one person said something or did something the other person didn't like, he would challenge that other person to a duel. When duels began, the fighters would not stop until one of them was killed. Some years later the swordsmen stopped if one person was clearly winning. Today people fight with swords just for sport.

The idea of fencing is to "fence off" the times when a player tries to spear his opponent. *(Demonstrate thrust.)* A player moves his sword to the side and uses it to keep his opponent's sword from touching him. Today in the sport of fencing, the fencers have rubber tips on the end of their swords. They only have to touch the other person to get a point. When players fight a bout in the sport of fencing, the opponents are not enemies. Also both players are still alive and well when they finish even though one is a loser.

Long ago the children of Israel used swords as weapons. Goliath, you remember, had a very big sword. King Saul had a sword and Joshua had a sword. All of these swords were used for war.

You can have a sword today too. Do you know what it is? Listen to the seventeenth verse of Ephesians, chapter six: "And take the helmet of salvation, and the sword of the Spirit, which is the word of God." The sword you have to win your battles over sin is the Bible.

Do your remember when Jesus was in the wilderness and Satan came to tempt Him? Each time Jesus would answer, "It is written . . ." and He would use a verse from the Bible. The sword of the Spirit worked, for Jesus won over Satan.

You too can use the Bible as your sword! If Satan tempts you to sin, you can fight him off with God's Word. It's a lot better than this sword, *(hold it up again)* because the sword of the Holy Spirit guards you and with it you will surely win!

40
FOLLOW THE LEADER

OBJECT: The seal of the president or governor; a badge from a leader in the armed forces, or a paper crown.

CONCEPT: Choosing the right leader to follow is very important.

TEXT: *Luke 9:23* "... If any man would come after me, let him deny himself and take up his cross daily and follow me."

Most boys and girls like to play Follow the Leader. It really is a very easy game to learn. Let's just say that I'm the leader and you are the followers. Now you must say or do everything that I say or do. OK? We should try a few things just to see how good you all are at following. *(Try a few things like clapping your hands twice, put your hands over your ears, say a few short sentences, etc.)* You did very well.

Good followers always listen to the leader and do all that he tells them to do or say.

In almost every sport, each team must have a coach. The coach is the real leader. He is the one who makes the plans about how to play against the other team. The coach must know how to play the game very well so that he can explain it to the players. For instance, the coach might tell his basketball team of tall boys to shoot the ball a lot against a team that has mostly short players. The players must listen to the coach and play the way he wants them to play.

A king is like a coach. He wears a crown like this one *(hold up the paper crown for all to see)*. He must lead his people well. Like a coach, he must know what his people need to be safe and happy. He makes the important decisions and laws. The people then listen and follow him, or leave the country to follow another king or leader.

In the game *Follow the Leader,* there can be only one leader or everyone will get mixed up. In sports only one coach must make the important decisions about which play to use or the team will never win. Jesus is the only good leader for the Christian. Is Jesus the King of your life? *(Hold up crown.)* Is He the leader of your life? Be sure to follow Him.

41
AUTO RACING

OBJECT: A checkered flag

CONCEPT: God has a reward for all His faithful children.

TEXT: *Romans 6:23* "For the wages of sin is death but the free gift of God is eternal life. . . ."

Can you imagine what life was like before there were cars? Actually cars were invented less than a hundred years ago. Henry Ford made the first car around 1903. The first cars couldn't go very fast. People laughed because horses could go faster. Soon the cars were made better, and they had more powerful engines. Then races were held to see which car was the best. Some of the first car races had very low speeds. The fastest car could go only fifteen miles per hour.

Today cars can go much faster. Now race cars can go faster than two hundred miles per hour. In an automobile race all of the drivers try to go as fast as they can so they can finish the race first. Some races are five hundred miles long so the racers must go around and around and around the track. The drivers don't know just how many times they must still go around. They can't hear anything because the motors are roaring. The judges use flags to tell the drivers if they must go slowly because of an accident or if they can go fast. On the last lap or trip around the track, the judges wave a white flag. Then when the winner comes to the finish line, the judge waves a checkered flag like this one. *(Hold up the flag and wave it dramatically.)* The flag tells the driver that he has won and now the race is over. All of the other drivers know, too, that the race is finished. The winner then drives his car into the winner's circle and receives the trophy or prize for winning the race.

Do you remember the story of the rich man and Lazarus? Lazarus was very sick and poor. It looked like he had lost the race, but God called him to heaven. He got the checkered winner's flag and won eternal life. God gave him a great reward. Lazarus could live forever with God. The rich man wasn't called to heaven because he didn't love God. He really lost the race.

If we love Jesus, God promises that He will give us a reward, a prize, a trophy. Every Christian will be able to live forever with Jesus. We will always be happy in heaven. We will always be in the winner's circle. That is the best prize.

42
CHARADES

OBJECT: A badge of a policeman, a fireman's hat, or other such symbol of a profession.

CONCEPT: The things we do tell others a lot about what kind of people we are.

TEXT: *Colossians 4:5, 6* "Conduct yourselves wisely toward outsiders, making the most of the time. Let your speech always be gracious, seasoned with salt...."

I'm going to pretend that I'm doing something. I'm not going to tell you what it is. I want you to guess. Just watch what I do, and then tell me your guesses. *(You're a baseball pitcher. Pretend first that you have the ball in your hand, indicating approximately the size of the ball. Do a wind-up before the pitch and then pitch the imaginary ball. After a short pause pretend that you have caught the ball thrown back from the catcher. Go through the procedure again and this time pretend that the batter hits the ball and you watch it fly over your head.)* Now, who can guess what I was pretending to do? *(Accept pupil's guesses.)* Right! That wasn't so hard to guess, was it? *(If you have time you can act out other situations like driving a car or even brushing your teeth.)*

We have just played a little game called *Charades*. This is one of the oldest and most popular of the guessing games. We could play it here by picking two teams. One team would have to secretly pick out some word or thing or action and then act it out to see if the other team could guess what it is.

Look at this badge for just a minute. *(Hold up the badge for all to see.)* If you saw someone wearing this, you would be able to guess immediately what he does. Who can tell what person uses this badge? *(Let children respond.)* Right! A policeman! He wouldn't have to say anything and yet you would know right away just what he does. The badge tells you!

In the game of *Charades,* your actions make it easy for anybody to guess who you are pretending to be. By doing certain things, the others will know what you have in mind. Sometimes the things we wear also tell what we do.

If someone watches you, could he tell that you are a Christian? When you are with your friends at school or on the playground, your life is something like a game of *Charades.* What you do when you're with others, the way you act, is like a badge that tells immediately what kind of boy or girl you are.

If you use bad words or are mean to your brothers and sisters, you don't have to say anything. Everyone will know that you don't love Jesus very much. But if you're kind to your friends even when they're not kind to you, then they'll know you are really a Christian. They'll know you are not just acting or making believe like in a game of *Charades.*

TRACK

OBJECT: Stopwatch

CONCEPT: The Christian life is a race that requires much training and a stick-to-it attitude.

TEXT: *Hebrews 12:1* "Therefore, since we are surrounded by so great a cloud of witnesses, let us also lay aside every weight, and sin which clings so closely, and let us run with perseverance the race that is set before us."

In the early spring of the year, you may see some students running along the road or on the sidewalk. Usually they aren't running very fast. They just run steadily. Do you know why they do that? Well, in the spring, the track season opens, and these runners are getting in shape. By running regularly, they are building up their muscles, lungs, and hearts, making them strong for the time when the track meets are held.

At the track meet the judge uses a stopwatch like this one *(hold it up)*. When a race begins, the official pushes the little button here *(do so)* and the watch starts. The big hand goes around to show the seconds and the little hand here shows the minutes. *(Hold up the watch so the audience can see the hand turn and when the second hand gets to nine or ten seconds, push the button to stop.*) Now when I push this button, the watch stops. The official does this when the winning runner crosses the finish line. You see where it stopped? Just about nine to ten seconds. Well, 9.1 seconds is the world's record for a 100-yard race. Bob Hayes set that record. He ran 100 yards in less time than it took me to show you the stopwatch.

How do you suppose he could do that? Do you think he just decided one day to run the 100-yard dash that fast? You know better, don't you! You know he must have run and run and run for days and weeks, even months, to get ready for that race. In the days of the apostle Paul, when runners were getting ready to run a race, they would place weights on their legs and feet while they practiced. Then in the real race when they took the weights off, their feet would feel light, and they could run very fast.

Hebrews 12:1 tells us that we are to "... lay aside every weight, and the sin which doth so easily beset us, and let us run with patience the race that is set before us" (KJV).

At the track meet there are 100-yard and 220-yard races. But there are also longer races like the half mile and the mile. Some cross-country races are several miles. These long races take even more strength and endurance.

The Bible says that living the Christian life is like running such a long race. At a cross-country track meet, the runner may start out with lots of pep. He may run happily and swiftly for quite a distance, but if he starts to get tired and then more tired, should he just drop out? Not if he wants to win!

Living the Christian life means you have to stay in top spiritual condition. You have to lay aside the things that would keep you from doing your best for God's kingdom. The race isn't over yet. When will it end? Only when God, who knows all things, pushes the stopwatch and says, "That's far enough, now enter into the joy of the Lord." Until then, use every new day in God's service to His praise.

44
CHINESE CHECKERS

OBJECT: Chinese checker board with marbles in two opposing corners

CONCEPT: The devil has to get out of our hearts and God has to come in before we can live the Christian life as we should.

TEXT: *Romans 7:19* "For I do not do the good I want, but the evil I do not want is what I do."

Today I brought my Chinese checker board along. You can see I have the marbles all in place, and the game is ready to start. If I want to win, I have to move all of my marbles out of my corner and into the opposite corner. The problem is that the corner is now full of other marbles. Those marbles have to be moved out before I can move mine in. Now, let's see. I can't just move them all over there at once either. I have to go one move at a time. But I can jump like this *(move marble in second row out to the front line).*

The game of Chinese checkers is a good way to show what happens in our hearts when we grow and mature as Christians. First, we have to get all the evil thoughts and desires and ideas out of our hearts. God gives us a new heart when we are born again. Then we live day by day with our new hearts, we fill them with new thoughts, and new desires and new ideas—those that praise God. That doesn't happen all at once. Every day we can help to fill our hearts just a little more with good thoughts. That's like moving the marbles into our new corner, one by one.

When you play Chinese checkers, you may become so busy with the game and with your friends that you sometimes forget one marble. He gets left way back there in your old corner and there's nobody around to jump and help him along. Slowly he has to come out of your old corner, one move at a time. That takes a long time. He may even make you lose the game.

That sometimes happens in our hearts too. There's one little sin that gets left behind. Maybe we don't see it, or we just overlook it. Getting it out is a long, slow, hard trip. But if we are going to win the game, we have to get this sin out too. We have to get all of the evil ideas and thoughts out. When we get into our new corner, we can't quit playing until there are no more empty holes.

Our new hearts, our Christian hearts, will be just the opposite of what they were before we were Christians. They will be emptied of all those things that were against God. They will be filled with praise to God. Instead of hate, there will be love.

45
CROSS TAG

OBJECT: Three pupils and yourself for a game demonstration

CONCEPT: Jesus comes between the judgment of God and the sinner.

TEXT: *I Timothy 2:5* "For there is one God, and there is one Mediator between God and men, the man Christ Jesus."

Most boys and girls know how to play lots of different kinds of tag. In every kind of tag, there is one person who is *It*. He has to run after another player and catch him. When he touches that person, the person he touches becomes *It*. Then *It* has to catch someone else. If you play *Squat Tag*, the person who is being chased can squat down like this *(demonstrate)* and he is safe. Then the one who is "*It*" must chase someone else.

Today I'd like to tell you about *Cross Tag*. For this game I'll need three children to help me. *(Have children come up by you.)* It goes like this. Just suppose I was *It* and I was trying to catch *(John)*. *(Act like you are chasing him.)* Then if someone else like *(Jim)* ran between us *(have Jim do so)*, he would cross our paths and I would have to try to catch *(Jim)* instead. If while I was chasing *(Jim)*, somebody else like *(Mary)* would cross between us, I would have to try to catch her instead. *(Have a girl as well as boys share in the demonstration.)*

You see that if one runner is getting tired, his friend who is rested and fresh can save him from being caught by crossing between him and the person who is *It*. The person who is *It* then has to chase a new runner instead. *(At this point thank the children and have them return to their seats.)*

Did you ever stop to think about how cross tag works? If you're almost caught, someone can save you by crossing between you and *It*. Then he will be chased for doing so.

God's plan of salvation works something like that game. Because we are sinners, God's judgment will surely catch us. But before it does, Jesus comes. He comes between God's judgment and us, so we can go free.

Do you know why Jesus can do this? He loved us so much that He died on the cross for us! All of the pain and punishment for sin was borne by Jesus. He is the only one who can cross between us and God and save us from eternal death.

In the game of Cross Tag, sometimes it is too late for a friend to cross between, and the runner gets caught. If you want Jesus to cross between, to save you from your sins, you have to ask Him to do so. You mustn't wait until it's too late!

46
TABLE TENNIS

OBJECT: Paddle and ball

CONCEPT: When you try to play the edge, there is a real danger you may fall off.

TEXT: *Psalm 37:27* "Depart from evil, and do good; so shall you abide forever."

Isn't this a nice paddle I have in my hand? *(Hold it up for all to see.)* Do you know what kind of game it's used for? *(Solicit some answers from group.)* Yes, it's a table tennis paddle. Some people call it Ping-Pong. In fact, the game was first called Ping-Pong when it started in the year 1880. There was even a Ping-Pong Association that started in 1902. Today the game is officially called table tennis.

The ball is hollow and it weighs only 2½ grams. It bounces very easily. Just watch *(bounce the ball on your paddle several times).*

Chang Tse-tung from China was the world champion table tennis player for several years. When he would smash *(demonstrate smashing stroke)* the ball against his opponent, the ball would travel over sixty miles an hour.

When you play table tennis, you must hit the ball across the net. If the ball lands right in the middle of the other side of the table, it will be quite easy for your opponent to hit it back. When you get a little better at playing, you can make the ball land just on the edge of the table. That takes quite a bit of skill, because sometimes you miss. The ball goes too far, it goes out of bounds, and your opponent gets a point.

Getting too close to the edge of the table in table tennis may be risky. Do you know that some people live risky lives? They ask, "What does the law say?" If the law says fifty-five miles an hour is the top speed limit for a car, they may go fifty-six or fifty-seven because they think they won't get stopped if they are so close to what the law permits. They are just on the edge of being stopped by the police.

Or they know the Bible says we must not lie. They tell part of the truth but don't tell quite the whole truth. Again they stay right on the edge.

The Bible also says that we must honor our father and mother. Sometimes a parent will ask a child to do something. The boy or girl will wait until mother or father says it again. He waits just as long as he dares, and then does the task only to avoid punishment. This is also living just on the edge of what is right or wrong.

If you live right on the edge, you are in danger of falling off. Just as in table tennis, you may miss the edge and do what's wrong instead of right. Stay away from the edge. Work to do what is clearly right.

47
SWIMMING

OBJECT: A goldfish in a small fish bowl
CONCEPT: It ought to be as natural for a Christian to pray as it is for a fish to swim.
TEXT: *I Thessalonians 5:17* "Pray without ceasing" (KJV).

Look what I have here! *(Hold up the goldfish bowl and show the fish.)* It's a goldfish, swimming in a bowl. Swimming is supposed to be one of the best kind of exercises. When you swim, you have to turn your head from one side to the other as you swing your arms *(demonstrate)* and kick your legs. Watch this little fish swim for a minute. He waves just one little fin, and he sails clear across his pool. If he wants to dart across, he flicks his tail, and zips away. When I watch him, I think, "Boy, I wish I could swim like that."

Maybe you have watched on TV the Olympic swimming teams as they raced back and forth across the pool. Maybe you said, "I wish I could swim like that."

To swim like that takes practice, long hours of regular practice to develop the skill and the endurance that is needed.

There are lots of other things that take practice, too. One of them is praying.

Praying isn't always easy is it? For some ministers, the prayer is the hardest part of the church service. Sometimes a person is asked to offer a prayer at a meeting and he may find it hard to do. If your teacher tells you that it is your turn to pray in class tomorrow or next week, you can get ready for that prayer time. You can think of the things you need to pray for, but you can also pray. The more you pray, the easier it is to pray. Listen to what Paul says in I Thessalonians 5:17, "Pray without ceasing." That means we should pray much. For the Christian, talking to God in prayer ought to be as natural as swimming is to a goldfish.

48
ROVER,
RED ROVER

OBJECT: Several children to come up and hold hands with you and one to call and run through the line.

CONCEPT: We sometimes ask people to join the church but we often fail to make them feel as welcome as we should if they do come.

TEXT: *Romans 15:7* "Welcome one another, therefore, as Christ has welcomed you. . . ."

Today we're going to talk about a game that some of you children probably play at school. It's called, *Rover, Red Rover.* Do any of you know how to play it? *(If several children raise their hand, have them come up; otherwise, select about eight or ten children. Have about half of them join you to form a line and the others should form the opposing line with enough space between so the runner has a little way to go.)* Will you come to play the game with me? Why don't about four of you hold hands with me on this side and the rest make a line on the other side of the platform facing us.

We want to be sure we have a good tight hold of each other's hands, because when we call for someone to come over, that person will have to run over here and try to get through our line. And if he does, he can take somebody back with him; but if he can't get through, he has to stay with us.

Let's try it. Let's see who shall we ask for? *(Hold a conference with members of your team and agree on one member of the other side.)* Now let's all call him together:

Rover, Red Rover.

Let *(child's name)* come over.

(This person runs across and tries to break through your line. If he doesn't get through, he must stay. If he gets through he chooses someone to take back with him.)

Now it's your turn to call for someone from our side, *(this may continue if you have time)* but, because we don't have too much time, I'm going to ask you to take your seats again and think with me about that game.

Do you know what we did? We asked *(child's name)* to come to our side. We gave her an invitation to join us, didn't we? We said, *(child's name)*, come over. And then when she came, you know what we did? We didn't hold out our hands to welcome her, we just held our own hands and she had to run and push hard to even get in.

That happens in church and Sunday school sometimes, too. We want people to come. We say, "Come to church and join us." But then if they do decide to come, you know what sometimes happens? We don't hold out our hands to welcome them. We just hold on to our own group of friends, and the newcomer almost has to push his way in to join us.

A tight line of friends is needed for a game of *Rover, Red Rover.* But when strangers come to our church, and new boys and girls come to Sunday school, let's have our hands out to welcome them.

49
SACK RACE

OBJECT: A few empty sacks

CONCEPT: Getting tangled up with the things of this world can keep you from progressing in your Christian faith.

TEXT: *II Timothy 2:4* "No man that warreth entangleth himself with the affairs of this life; that he may please him who hath chosen him to be a soldier" (KJV).

You know what I have here? *(Hold up the sacks).* These are empty sacks. They were maybe used to hold *(look at label and read what it says or if they have no label say . . .)* corn or wheat. Today I'd like to have a few boys come up to show how you can use them for a special kind of race—a sack race! Let's have three boys come up to show how this works! *(Get three outgoing volunteers.)* Good! Now two of you just get inside your sacks and let's start here *(indicate a starting line in the aisle)* and go to here *(indicate a finish line within the limits of your space and time).* Now when I say "Go," run as fast as you can. Let's see who can get there first. (Note: *two of the boys are in sacks; the third is not).* On your mark! Ready; Set; Go! _____

was first, _____ was second, and _____ was third. That was fine! Thank you for helping me today. *(Lay aside sacks and have boys return to their seats.)*

Did you notice something while that race was going on? One boy, _____, had his legs free, so he won easily. The other boys couldn't run like they usually do. No, they hopped and took little steps instead. It took longer for them because their feet weren't free to stretch out for big steps. If they would try to take big steps, they would soon fall down because their feet would get all tangled up in the sack.

Christians are running a race too—the race of life. If they get all tangled up in the things of this world, they will really get slowed down. Jesus said it was very hard for a rich man to enter into heaven. He said Christians should be more like the lilies of the field and the birds of the air that depend entirely on God for their needs. God doesn't want us to get too involved with food, clothes, bikes, cars, and other such things. He doesn't want us to get so tangled up with things that we forget where we're really going.

In one of the parables, the Parable of the Sower, Jesus told about seed that fell on good ground and produced much fruit. He also told about some plants that started to grow up and then got all tangled up with weeds and tares. They got choked out and couldn't produce fruit. He said these tares and thorns were the cares of the world and the delights of riches.

You boys and girls hear the Word of God, too, in church and Sunday school. The seed of the Word is planted in your heart. But if you get all tangled up with the things of this world, you won't be able to grow very much as a Christian. You won't be able to produce much fruit for Jesus. That's like trying to run a race with your feet in a sack. You may get there. You may hop and stumble to the finish line, but it's going to slow you down! Don't get all tangled up, Christians!

50
JUMP ROPE

OBJECT: A child's jump rope

CONCEPT: A regular schedule of prayer and Bible study is the best for spiritual growth.

TEXT: *I Corinthians 15:58* "Therefore, my beloved brethren, be steadfast, immovable, always abounding in the work of the Lord. . . ."

Here is something most girls and a lot of boys enjoy playing with. It's a jump rope. Most of you know how this works, but just in case you don't, let me show you. You just swing the rope over your head like this *(do so)* and when it gets down by your feet you jump up *(do so)* and the rope goes underneath and on around again.

The thing you have to do if you want to jump rope well, is to get a rhythm started. Once I watched some children jumping rope. They were good at it. You know what they were doing at the same time? They were singing little songs. The songs would set the rhythm so the timing would be just right. They could keep right on swinging and jumping, and they hardly ever missed. It seemed to go so smoothly and easily.

God has set many rhythms in the world around us. The sun

comes up and the sun goes down. The tide at the seashore comes in and the tide goes out; spring follows winter and summer follows spring. These are some of the smooth rhythms of nature.

A smooth rhythm is important for the Christian life too. God started that smooth rhythm when He first made the world. In six days He created all things. He set aside the seventh day as a day of rest and worship. Round and round the weeks seem to go and if a Christian misses church on Sunday, the rhythm is broken. It's like tripping on the rope.

There are other kinds of rhythm in the Christian life, too. One very important rhythm is the times we have for prayer and the times we set aside to read the Bible. We get into a smooth rhythm of praying at mealtimes and bedtime. If we do this regularly, our Christian life grows steadily. But when we skip those times, something happens. It's just like jumping rope; the rhythm breaks. Of course, we can start again, but sometimes it takes a little while before we're going smoothly.

There's a rhythm to the way we learn too. Suppose your Sunday school teacher had five lessons in a row about the story of Daniel. You came to class for the first three lessons and then you skipped lesson four and came again for lesson five. Or, suppose you came only for lessons two, three, and five. You would miss part of the Bible story, wouldn't you? Or, suppose you were going to read the Gospel of Matthew in the Bible and you read chapters 1, and 2, and 3, and then you jumped to chapter 6. You would miss part of the story of Jesus' life.

Coming to Sunday school, reading the Bible, and praying are a little like jumping rope. Do them regularly and the rhythm is smooth and you will steadily feel that Jesus is a closer friend. But if you start missing Sunday school once in a while; if you start missing reading the Bible and praying regularly, your Christian growth gets jerky, it may even stop for awhile. God's Word tells us to be "steadfast."